The One Minute Investor

A Guide for the Individual Investor
2nd Edition

Robert B. Clayton, CFP®, CLU, ChFC

Bloomington, IN  Milton Keynes, UK

authorHOUSE™

AuthorHouse™
1663 Liberty Drive, Suite 200
Bloomington, IN 47403
www.authorhouse.com
Phone: 1-800-839-8640

AuthorHouse™ *UK Ltd.*
500 Avebury Boulevard
Central Milton Keynes, MK9 2BE
www.authorhouse.co.uk
Phone: 08001974150

This book is a work of non-fiction. Unless otherwise noted, the author and the publisher make no explicit guarantees as to the accuracy of the information contained in this book and in some cases, names of people and places have been altered to protect their privacy.

First published by AuthorHouse   3/14/2006

ISBN: 1-4259-1502-7 (sc)

Printed in the United States of America
Bloomington, Indiana

This book is printed on acid-free paper.

Foreword.....

Americans spend more time planning their vacations than they do planning their finances!

The purpose of this book is to provide concise, pragmatic information to the consumer which shows not only what basic products are available, but also the relative level of risk associated with each one, and to enable the reader to develop his own investment plan.

It's important to realize that all investments involve some degree of risk. Therefore the investor must decide how much risk he is willing to assume, and whether or not it will be sufficient enough to permit him to achieve his financial objectives.

Obviously, the title of this book is an oxymoron! It takes years of study and experience to become a savvy investor. However, this book, designed to be a starting point, will help the reader to explore some of the fundamentals of investing.

Robert B. Clayton, CFP®, CLU, ChFC

A Special Thanks

to

Megan A. McGuire

Table of Contents

There are only a few basic concepts that you need to understand in order to invest money effectively. Let's briefly discuss each one.

Why You Should Invest

When it comes to money, most people consider themselves to be either "savers" or "investors". Savers are concerned about protecting their principal, while investors are primarily concerned about protecting their money's purchasing power.

The purpose of investing is really to do both: protect your principal and protect the *purchasing power* of your money. Protecting your money's purchasing power is necessary because of inflation. The cost of goods and services is continually rising, which not only shrinks the value of your money, but in effect, reduces the amount of goods that you're able to purchase.

All investors face "inflation risk" which is the chance that your investment returns may not outpace the rate of inflation. In addition, you also have to pay taxes on your earnings unless you are using a tax-free or tax-deferred investment. What's important to the investor is your **real rate of return**. This is your net return after you take into consideration both inflation and taxes (the enemies of wealth creation).

Investing effectively should enable you to reduce the negative effects of inflation and taxes on your money by producing investment results which over time will exceed both the inflation rate and your tax bracket rate.

Below is the calculation for figuring your **real rate of return** on a $10,000 one year certificate of deposit. On the following page is a graph which illustrates the impact of inflation on one dollar from 1970 to 2005.

Calculating your real rate of return on a $10,000
one year certificate of deposit

$10,000 1 Year CD @ 5%	=	$500.00 CD Interest Earnings
28% Tax Bracket	= -	$140.00 Tax on Earnings
3 ½ % Inflation Rate	= -	<u>$368.00</u> Inflation
		(Principal and Interest)
Real Rate of Return		<$8.00>

What does this mean to you? The time has come when you can no longer afford to keep all or the majority of your money in traditional banking or fixed income type products. The long term negative effects of inflation and taxes are too severe.

Don't be misled to think that inflation has gone away. The rising cost of goods and services is sometimes difficult to detect due to the volatility in prices. Just think about it… are you paying more for items today than you were 4–5 years ago? The answer is "yes"! Inflation is alive and well. Typically, the cost of goods doubles every twenty years.

The prudent investor needs to diversify and seek alternative investments with at least a portion of his money. This will help to provide a hedge against inflation.

The Impact of Inflation

Since 1970 the purchasing power of the dollar has declined more than 80%

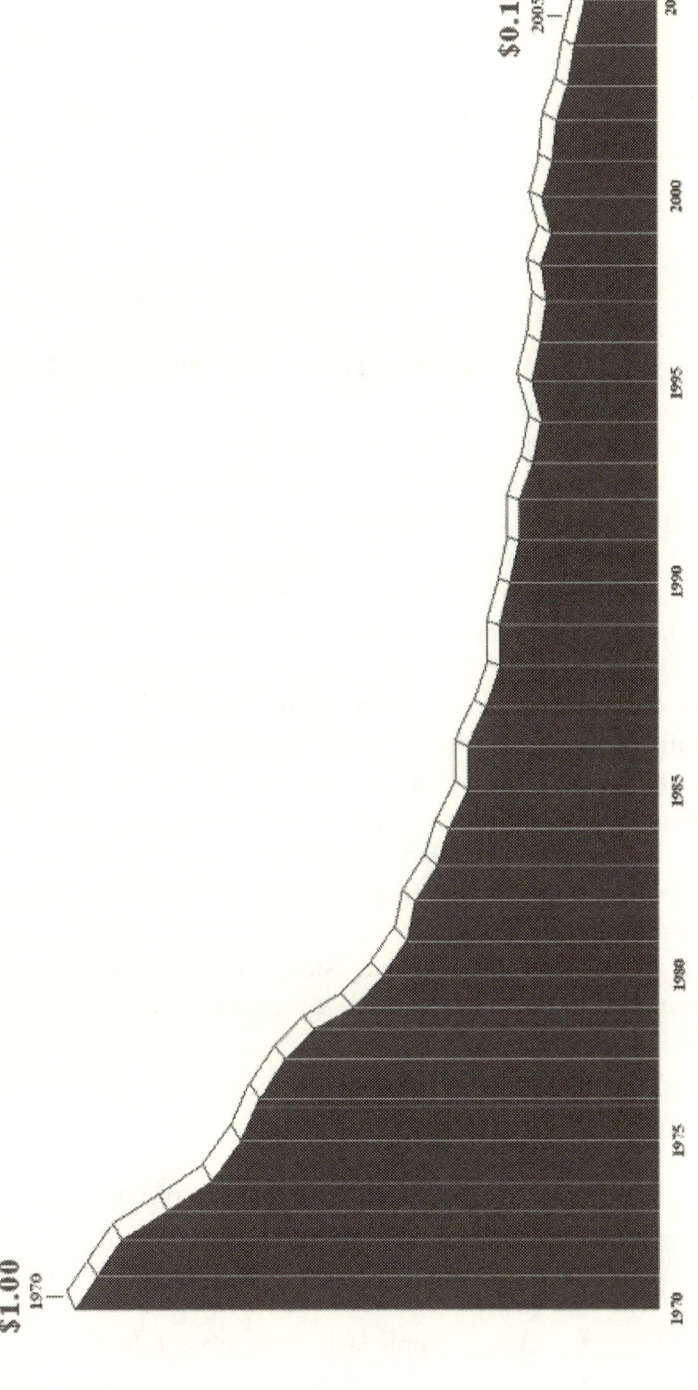

Determine Your Investment Plan

The most important aspect of investing is to have a plan which will enable you to determine financially where you are now, where you want to go, strategies for how to get there, and periodic reviews for maximizing results.

When you think about it, having a plan is the most important concept for accomplishing any objective. Could you imagine starting on your vacation without a plan, or a football coach starting to play an opponent without a game plan? Absolutely not! So, why should your finances be any different? A plan doesn't have to be long or complicated in order to be effective. It simply outlines what you want to accomplish and provides a strategy for action.

Surveys have revealed that the one trait all highly successful people have in common is that they set goals and have a specific plan of action to accomplish those goals.

Once a plan has been established, each investment must be evaluated in terms of how well it fits within the overall plan.

Why do people fail to establish a plan? There are four (4) common reasons:

- They don't realize the importance of a plan relative to achieving their goals;
- Some fear failure, by not being able to accomplish their goals;
- Others simply lack commitment; however,
- Most people just don't know how to get started.

With this in mind, let's outline the process for developing an investment plan.

Clearly Define Your Investment Objectives

Financially, what is it exactly that you want to achieve? Do you want to accumulate money for a vacation? A new car? A new home? Your children's college education? Retirement?

The first step is to write down all of your objectives, and then you need to prioritize them in order of importance. You might not be able to work on all of them at one time due to financial limitations. It's usually best to focus on them one at a time.

Next, divide your goals into short term, intermediate, and long term. Even though there is no set timetable for these periods of time, most commonly, short term goals would be those that you would want to accomplish within a year or less, like planning an annual vacation. Intermediate goals would be those that are to be achieved within 2-3 years, such as purchasing a new car. While long term goals would be those to be completed in five (5) years or more. This would include accumulating money for the children's college expenses, purchasing a new home, and planning for retirement. If your objective is retirement planning, remember to coordinate your investments with your retirement plan at work if possible.

In order to substantially improve your chances of achieving these objectives, as you are writing them down, make sure that each one:

- Is defined in a specific and measurable manner, avoid vague and ambiguous language;
- Is both realistic and achievable for your financial situation;
- Has a definite time parameter for being completed; and
- Has a plan of action or strategy detailing how to proceed and exactly what needs to be done.

Figure Out Where You Are Now In Relation To Achieving Those Goals

One of the best ways to access your present financial position is by calculating your net worth. This will provide you with a starting point. Your net worth is similar to a financial inventory representing your ability to convert assets into income. It is also similar to a corporation's balance sheet. It gives you a static look at your current financial situation as if everything you own was converted into cash and then used to pay off all your debt.

Ideally, your net worth should increase each year. Net worth is calculated by subtracting your liabilities (everything you owe) from your assets (everything you own). See worksheet II entitled Net Worth Calculation.

Ascertain What Resources You Have for Investing

The easiest way to accomplish this is by examining your monthly budget. If you don't have one, you'll need to establish one. Unfortunately, some people tend to think of a budget in negative terms. It is perceived as being restrictive. However, a more positive approach would be to view it as a "spending" plan. Because in reality, a budget is nothing more than planned spending. Many people have no idea *how* they spend their money. When they make an analysis of their cash flow, they are usually quite surprised at the amount of money they waste.

From your budget you can not only analyze your monthly inflow and outflow of funds, but also uncover potential sources of money for investing.

A good way to proceed is to calculate your cash flow (see worksheet III-Monthly Surplus Calculation). By completing the monthly surplus calculation, you'll be able to ascertain if you're spending: more than you earn (by using credit, maybe you've created a monthly deficit); all that you earn (at the end of each month you have no money left); or less than you earn (at month's end you'll have some money left over).

Regardless of your situation, you'll benefit by finding ways to reduce your monthly expenses and/or credit card debt and start systematically accumulating money for investing. The primary objective is to spend LESS than you bring home each month. Doing this will enable you to create a positive cash flow.

If you have no accumulated money, here are some ideas to help you start setting aside money on a regular basis:

- Divide your expenses into "needs" and "wants". A need is something that you can't live without, such as food and water. However, there are ways to reduce the money being spent in this area, like using discount coupons, planning your meals before shopping, avoid shopping when you're hungry, and buying certain food items only when they are on sale. A want is a luxury. Eliminate as many of these as you can (at least temporarily). A good example would be a cell phone. You *can* live without it. At the very least, consider reducing all the "bells and whistles". These extras increase the cost dramatically. Notice how things once considered *luxuries* are now considered *necessities*;
- Pay yourself <u>first</u> each month. Literally write yourself a check and deposit it into your savings account;
- Track your spending for four (4) consecutive weeks. Write down daily <u>everything</u> on which you spend money. Have each family member do this. Analyze your findings every week. Identify and eliminate wasteful spending;
- Rent movies instead of going out;
- Eliminate purchasing daily snacks, soft drinks, potato chips, and candy bars from vending machines;
- Consider taking your lunch to work;
- Contact the local electric company. Have them schedule an energy inspection at your residence and provide you with ideas on how to conserve energy;
- Pay cash (paper money) when you can for minor purchases. Accumulate all change (coins) daily and deposit monthly into your savings account;
- Clean out your garage, closets, and basement. Collect all unnecessary items and have a yard sale. This is a fast way to gather cash and jump-start your investment program. Whatever items you don't sell, donate to charity;

- Change to "basic" cable T.V. service and eliminate the expense of all extra add-ons;
- Shop around and find the best rate for your auto and homeowners insurance at least one month prior to the renewal date;
- Carpool to work with family or friends whenever possible. This is a great way to save money, especially with the high cost of gasoline; and
- If you have credit card debt, analyze each statement and question unauthorized charges and/or fees. Always pay more than the minimum required monthly payment if possible, otherwise with a high finance charge, it could take you as long as 18 years or more to pay off the debt. If credit card debt is a major issue, consider a part-time second job until you can get it under control.

Getting a handle on your finances requires a major effort on your part, it won't happen automatically. It will take both sacrifice and self-discipline. It doesn't happen over-night… it takes time.

Establish the Parameters for Your Investments

a) Time Horizon -   Exactly when will you need the money? Make sure the investments you select coincide with your timetable for needing the money.

b) Moral Issues -   Is investing in companies that produce alcohol and tobacco products acceptable?

c) Liquidity/
Marketability -   How rapidly could you get to your money if you needed it? Would there be any potential loss?

d) Tax Consequences -	Are the earnings on your investment taxable, tax-deferred, or tax-free?
e) Diversification -	Does the investment provide diversification to your overall portfolio? Is the investment itself diversified?

Calculate Your Risk Tolerance Level

How much risk are you willing to take? How aggressive do you want to be? One way to obtain a good prospective of your risk tolerance level is by answering the questions in a risk tolerance profile questionnaire, such as the one on page 34.

Select and Purchase Specific Investments

This is the *most important step*, as nothing will be accomplished if you don't TAKE action! Allocate your money among the investment categories using the conservative, moderate, or aggressive approach percentages as a guide. Choose investments which would be appropriate based on your risk tolerance level and stated parameters. To help make your selections, refer to the basic investments in the Investment Pyramid on page 12.

Review Your Investments At Least Annually

Don't be hesitant to make the necessary changes and modifications as often as your personal situation dictates.

Generally, the younger you are the more risk you are able to accept. However, as you grow older, you may want to modify your investments to reflect a more conservative approach.

Major Investment Categories

Once you have accumulated some money or have money on a regular basis to invest, the next step is to decide how to invest it. There are only three major investment categories (see pyramid below). The first is the "Cash and Cash Equivalents" category, commonly referred to as capital preservation. This area, designed for liquidity and safety, includes short-term treasury securities (T-Bill), money market accounts, and traditional banking products: checking accounts, savings accounts, and short-term certificates of deposit.

The second category is "Income". As the name implies, this category's objective is to provide current income for the investor. This includes bonds, government agency mortgages, fixed-annuities, and government securities.

The third is the "Growth" category. This primarily includes equities and real estate, which provide the potential for capital appreciation and the opportunity to obtain investment returns that can over time consistently beat the inflation rate and your tax rate.

In addition to the growth objective, notice that the growth category has a "growth and income" objective which consists of products that not only provide income, but also have the potential for capital appreciation, as well as a "special situations" objective for the more aggressive and speculative investments.

The categories are usually seen in the form of an "Investment Pyramid". The following illustration shows the investment pyramid structure. Please note that the investment "objectives" are listed on the left side of the pyramid.

The Investment Pyramid
Key to Diversification

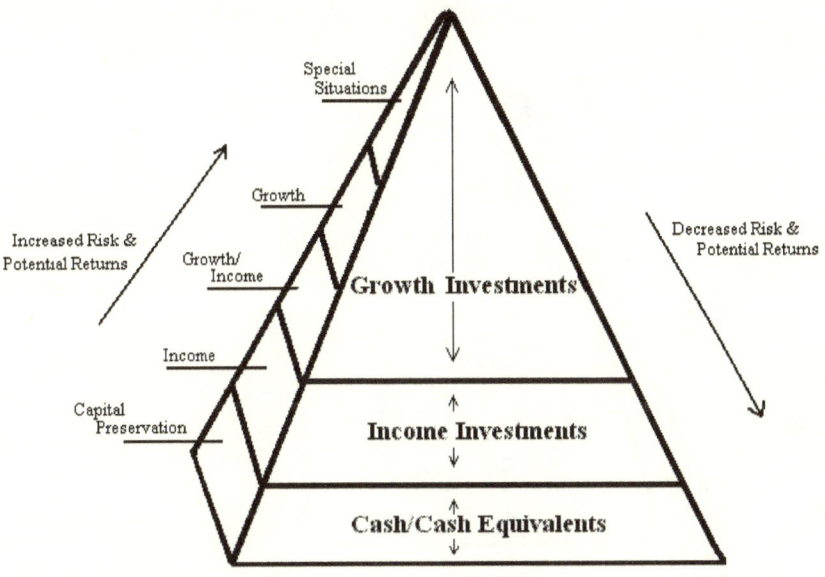

The Three Major Categories

Within these major categories there are numerous selections available. The following page illustrates the basic investments by category.

The Investment Pyramid

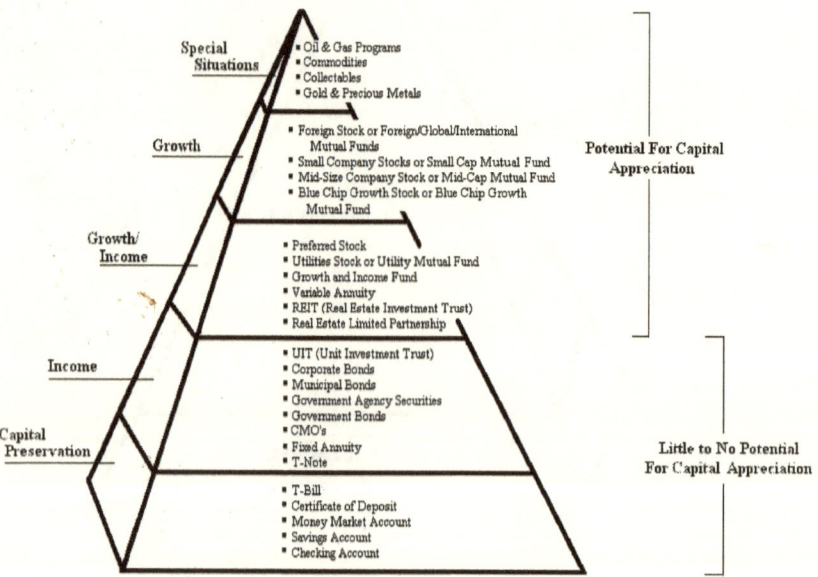

Basic Investments by Category

Basic Investments

This chapter will briefly discuss and give an overview for basic investments in the income, growth and income, growth, and special situation categories.

Investments for "Income"

Collateralized Mortgage Obligations
(CMO)

The CMO is a special type of security introduced into the marketplace in the early 1980's by the Federal Home Loan Mortgage Corporation (Freddie Mac). CMO's, now issued by banks, mortgage bankers, homebuilders, and investment banking firms, have become a very popular investment.

The Collateralized Mortgage Obligation is a multi-class pay-through security backed by the cash flow generated from a pool of high grade mortgages. Unlike the regular pay-throughs where there is only one maturity date, CMO's are issued in several different classes (generally 5), each having its own rate of interest and maturity date, which can range anywhere from 3 to 30 years.

In the regular mortgage pools, the payment of principal is paid on a pro rata basis, but CMO payments of principal are prioritized according to different classes. What's unique about a CMO is that the income stream produced includes both principal and interest. This is unlike the bond; which provides an interest only income and returns the full principal at maturity.

Frequently, a CMO may be "callable". This means that the issuer has the option to return the investor's principal before the actual maturity date.

Securities of the United States Government

The U.S. Government issues three types of marketable securities to fund its activities and help finance the national debt: the treasury bill, treasury note, and treasury bond.

A treasury bill (T-bill) has the maturity range from 1 month to 1 year. The minimum face value amount is $10,000 with additional $1,000 increments available. Issued at a discount, they are non-interest bearing. For example, an investor that purchases a 6 month T-bill for $9,700 will receive $10,000 at maturity. This is found in the capital preservation category. Most T-bills have a 4, 13, or 26 week maturity.

A treasury note (T-note) is issued with a maturity range from 2 to 10 years. Its lowest face amount is $1,000, but normally, there is a minimum purchase of five at most brokerage firms. Interest is paid every six months.

The treasury bond, also issued with a minimum face amount of $1,000, has maturities ranging up to 30 years. As with all bonds, interest is paid semi-annually. Both the treasury note and treasury bond are designed to provide income.

Since these securities are issued by the United States Government, they are automatically AAA rated and considered very safe. However, because of this, the yields are relatively low. If an investor holds a treasury note or treasury bond until its maturity, there is no risk to the principal involved. If the securities are sold prior to the maturity date, then there is a chance for possible loss or gain of principal. This is because they are interest sensitive and fluctuate in value with the rise and fall of general interest rate movement. If interest rates move downward, then their value increases and vice versa.

Government Agency Securities

These are securities issued on pools of mortgages. The fixed-rate, conventional, 30-year mortgages represent the largest class of mortgage-backed certificates. To entice the investor to purchase a pro rata interest in the mortgage pool, the originating financial institution will seek an agency to guarantee that the investor will receive the monthly payment of principal and interest regardless of whether or not the homeowner defaults in making payments.

There are three Federal Agencies that will guarantee payments for pass-through security investors:

- The Government National Mortgage Association (GNMA-commonly known as the Ginnie Mae);
- The Federal National Mortgage Association (FNMA-commonly known as Fannie Mae); and
- The Federal Home Loan Mortgage Corporation (FHLMC-commonly known as Freddie Mac).

Each of these agencies buys residential mortgages from lenders, consolidates them into a pool, issues securities based on the pool, and offers these securities to the general public.

Since most mortgage-backed securities are sold in round lots of one million dollars or more, far above the limits of the average individual investor, they are normally purchased by brokerage firms and divided into smaller denominations to make them more easily accessible. The Ginnie Mae mortgage is the only one that is a direct obligation of the U.S. Government. It may be purchased in $25,000 minimums and provides a monthly distribution. The only caveat is that each month the payment contains both interest and principal.

Mortgages typically yield more than treasuries and are designed primarily for those who need income.

Municipal Bonds

A bond is a debt obligation which must be repaid. Issuing bonds is a method of raising capital. There are three types of bonds: government, corporate, and municipal. Our focus in this section will be on municipal bonds.

Municipal bonds are issued by cities, counties, and municipalities. They are free from federal taxation. One question that investors ask frequently is whether or not they should consider purchasing or switching their current taxable investments into tax-free investments. The answer is determined by two factors: your investment objectives and your marginal income tax rate.

Assuming that a tax-free investment could fit into the parameters of your investment objectives, the next step is to figure out whether or not it offers an acceptable return relative to what yield is available in a taxable investment.

There is a formula which will help you to analyze tax-free yields. Simply divide the tax-free yield by 1.00 minus your marginal tax rate. This converts the tax-free yield into its taxable equivalent yield. Here's an example. Suppose that you are in the 28% income tax bracket and you want to purchase a municipal bond yielding 5%. Is this a prudent decision? To calculate the taxable equivalent yield, divide 5 (tax-free yield) by .72 (1.00-.28).

$$5\% \div .72 = 6.94\%$$
(tax-free yield)   (1.00-tax rate)   (taxable equivalent yield)

The result would be 6.94%. This means that you would have to find a taxable investment such as a certificate of deposit paying 6.94% in order to receive the same after-tax return that the municipal bond yielding 5% would provide. Municipal bonds become more attractive the higher your marginal income tax rate.

You could also use a variation of this formula to determine the tax-free equivalent yield if you knew the taxable yield. For example... if you could purchase a bank CD yielding 7%, what would be the yield after taxes, or the tax-free equivalent yield? In this case, multiply the taxable yield (7%) by 1.00 minus your tax rate. Assume a 28% tax bracket rate.

$$7\% \times .72 = 5.04\%$$
(taxable yield)   (1.00-.28)   (tax-free equivalent yield)

This means that a municipal bond paying 5.04% would provide the same after-tax return as a bank CD yielding 7% if you were in the 28% marginal income tax bracket.

Until recently, municipal bonds were the only true "tax-free" investment. Now, the Roth IRA is available to those with earned income and it is also tax-free. The big advantage is that Roth IRA contributions may be invested into equities, which will allow the investor the potential for tax-free growth via capital appreciation, something muni bonds aren't designed to do. The disadvantage is the annual contribution to a Roth IRA is limited. Also, it is not currently available to those with annual incomes over $110,000 if single and $160,000 if married.

Municipal bonds may be purchased individually, in a unit trust, or in a mutual fund. Before purchasing muni bonds, be sure that they are "investment grade" in quality. This means that the bonds are ranked in one of the four top bond rating categories. Bonds are rated in an effort to help investors determine the risk associated with the bond offering. *Moody's Investor Service* and *Standard & Poor's Corporation* are the two most common rating companies. The highest bond rating is AAA.

One technique that you might want to consider for enhancing your returns is to ladder or stagger the bonds' maturity dates, since normally the longer the maturity, the higher the yield. Everyone's tax situation is unique and dynamic, so it is suggested that you consult your tax advisor prior to making a decision to invest in tax-free investments.

Corporate Bonds

A corporate bond is a corporation's written pledge to repay a specified amount of money with interest at a designated time. Corporations issue bonds to avoid diluting company ownership. The minimum face amount is $1,000. Designed for income, they pay interest semi-annually. Here is how a bond works. Let's say an investor purchases ten 20-year corporate bonds at par (a thousand dollar face amount) with a coupon at 7%. That means the cost will be $10,000 plus commissions. Every six months, for twenty years, the investor will receive a check for $350. At the end of twenty years, the principal (initial investment) of $10,000 will be returned to the investor.

Bonds may be secured or unsecured. A debenture is a type of bond that is backed only by the reputation of the issuer. A mortgage or equipment trust bond is secured by various assets of the issuing corporation. A subordinate debenture is an unsecured bond that gives the bondholder a claim secondary to that of all other creditors with respect to both principal and interest. The coupon (rate of interest) of the bond is higher as the risk increases.

A corporation has two methods of ensuring that it will have sufficient funds available at maturity to redeem a bond issue:

- It may establish a sinking fund. This is a side fund into which deposits would be made on a regular basis; or
- It may issue serial bonds. These are bonds of a single issue that mature at different times.

Bonds may be purchased at "par" (thousand dollar face amount), at a "discount" (less than face amount), or at a "premium" (greater than face amount). Some bonds have a "call" feature which allows them to be "called in" or purchased from the bondholder prior to the maturity date. Be careful when purchasing bonds with a call feature, especially if they are selling at a premium.

Corporate bonds sometimes are "convertible". This means that they may be exchanged at the owner's option for a specified number of shares of the issuing corporation's common stock. Corporations like to issue convertible bonds, because they can be issued with a lower coupon, they attract more speculative investors, and if the convertible feature is exercised, they will no longer have to redeem it at maturity, which reduces company debt.

The Unit Investment Trust (UIT)

This is a unique investment for those seeking income. A unit investment trust is a registered investment company that buys and holds a portfolio of bonds, stock, or other securities. Instead of buying "shares" of a portfolio, <u>units</u> are sold at par for $1,000 each. There is a fixed number of units in each investment trust. There are two types of unit investment trusts: fixed-income and equity. The fixed is the most common and the one that we will discuss. Fixed income UITs commonly invest in municipal bonds, corporate bonds, government securities, or mortgages. Here's how it works. An investor purchases units of a UIT portfolio. This unmanaged portfolio can consist of 25 to 100 selected securities all of which have different yields and similar maturity dates. The UIT's maturity can range from 3 to 30 years. The stated termination date is based on the maturity dates of the securities in the trust. The yield will vary depending on the quality of the securities in the portfolio. The higher the quality, the lower the yield. The UIT can provide income on a monthly, quarterly, or semi-annual basis. As the securities within the portfolio mature, the UIT will diminish in both size and value. In addition to the interest, the investor will get back a portion of the original investment as each security matures and eventually the trust will be completely liquidated.

The units are interest sensitive and will fluctuate in value with the daily movement of interest rates. Therefore, when sold, units may be worth more or less than their original cost. Since units are redeemable, they may be sold at anytime.

Investments for "Growth and Income"

Real Estate Limited Partnership

A real estate limited partnership is a partnership that has at least one limited partner and one general partner. The limited partners generally have no liability beyond the amount of their investment. Consequently, they forfeit their right to participate in the control and management of the partnership. The general partners provide the management and have unlimited liability.

Partnerships have significant organizational and operational differences from REITs. Here are some of the major differences.

Partnerships:

- Usually offer the investor <u>no</u> liquidity. If any liquidity exists, it will be at a discount;
- Typically require a $2,000 - $5,000 minimum investment;
- Offer no reinvestment programs;

- Are controlled by the general partner, who can't be easily removed by the limited partners;
- Have no independent directors;
- Rarely have the ability to grow via additional public offerings of stock or debt;
- Do have the ability to pass losses on to investors;
- Provide schedule K-1 for investors instead of a 1099; and
- Subject investors to state taxes for all states in which it owns properties.

Be sure to do your homework before investing in real estate. Check out the track record of the property management group, including past performance of other offerings, as well as the credentials of its management team.

Real Estate Investment Trust
(REIT)

For the average investor, buying prime commercial real estate would be cost prohibitive. In 1960, the real estate investment trust (REIT) was created specifically to provide the small investor a way to invest in a pool of commercial properties or mortgages and derive an income. A REIT is an investment company that manages a portfolio of real estate in order to earn profits for its shareholders.

There are three types of REITs:

- <u>Equity</u> REITs which invest in real properties; (These are generally created for a finite period of time, during which the investor receives dividends on his investment and capital gains, if any, upon sale of the properties.);
- <u>Mortgage</u> REITs which invest in pooled money to finance construction loans and mortgages on developed properties; and
- <u>Hybrid</u> REITs which are a combination of mortgage and equity REITs.

Each REIT only offers a limited number of shares which are usually traded on stock exchanges or in the over-the-counter market. Federal law mandates that REITs distribute 90% of their net annual earnings to shareholders and refrain from engaging in speculative short-term real estate transactions for quick profits. REITs must have at least 100 shareholders, of which, no more than half of the shares may be owned by 5 or fewer people. In addition, they are required to hire independent real estate professionals to handle certain management activities.

The advantages to owning a REIT include: the potential for capital appreciation, thus providing a hedge against inflation; limited financial liability; a relatively small amount of money is needed for the initial purchase; it has none of the hassles associated with active management; and it provides both financial leverage and dividend income. Some disadvantages: certain REITs may be difficult to sell (about ⅓ of them aren't traded on an exchange); during economic cycles, their value will fluctuate; due to the Tax Reform Act of 1986, there is no longer a tax advantage for ownership; and sometimes management problems may develop.

All REITs are not created equal! You need to do a little research before investing. Equity REITs offer the investor the most appreciation potential and a high dividend with only moderate risk. The three main factors to consider before selecting a REIT are: debt level; growth record; and their property sales experience.

Annuities

An annuity is a financial contract written by an insurance company that provides the purchaser a regular income of periodic payments. The primary reason for purchasing an annuity is to receive a systematic income stream for life. The annuity is just the opposite of life insurance. It pays you while you are living. Life insurance pays when you die.

An annuity may be purchased with a lump sum of money with the income to begin at once. This is called an immediate annuity. It may also be purchased over time with the payments to begin at some future date. This is a deferred annuity. The amount of periodic payment received will be determined by several factors including gender, age, amount of money accumulated, and the pay-out option selected. Once the payments begin, they will last as long as you live even if the total paid out exceeds the amount of money accumulated. This is one important advantage of an annuity!

Many people use an annuity for their IRA or company retirement plan. Annual contributions to these *qualified* tax-deferred programs are limited. It is important to understand that money accumulated in a *non-qualified* annuity is also tax-deferred, but there is no maximum annual contribution. This is another advantage of an annuity.

If the annuitant (purchaser of the annuity) should die prior to beginning payments (annuitization), then the proceeds would automatically pass to the designated beneficiary and avoid probate. The death benefit is generally a guaranteed amount.

There are two types of annuities: fixed and variable. With a fixed annuity, the principal is guaranteed and the annuitant will receive a fixed amount of income each month for life. A variable annuity gives the investor the advantage of choosing how the accumulated money will be invested. Therefore, the monthly income may fluctuate depending on the performance of the investment options that are selected. There are many different variable annuity products on the market. Make sure you select one that is suitable for your situation, because there are various costs involved.

Most variable annuities offer "riders" that may be added by paying an additional premium. One of which allows the investor a way to participate in potential market gains without risk to their initial investment and guarantees at death a minimum of full return of principal to the beneficiary.

There is a variation of the fixed annuity called an equity indexed annuity. In addition to providing a fixed, guaranteed rate option, it also offers a yield based on the performance of a stock market index, such as the S&P 500.

Some of the other major advantages for purchasing an annuity include: tax-deferred accumulation/growth; probate avoidance; virtually unlimited annual contributions; it's creditor proof (in some states); and has flexible options available for receiving income.

Preferred Stock

Preferred Stock represents ownership in a corporation. It is typically for investors who need income, but want some growth potential. Preferred stock pays a guaranteed fixed dividend that is specified and determined in advance. Preferred stockholders have claim on a company's assets that is above that of the common stockholders. There are four types of preferred stock:

- cumulative preferred. Entitles its owner a continuous claim on company dividends, both past and present, even if suspended by the board of directors. Any unpaid dividends accumulate until the corporation resumes paying them. Cumulative preferred dividends must be paid before common stock dividends;
- non-cumulative preferred. The opposite of cumulative. It doesn't place a steady claim on dividends;
- participating preferred. Shareholders receive extra dividends over their normal ones when the company makes an extra profit and dividends are declared by the board of directors; and

- convertible preferred. Stock which may be converted into a certain number of common stock shares. Attractive to investors who want the opportunity to share in the appreciation of the company's common stock.

Preferred stock may carry a call provision. This entitles the issuing company to repurchase the stock from the shareholders. Although preferred stocked is normally called at par (face value), some call provisions actually pay a premium. Corporations use "calls" as a way to eliminate the payment of dividends, therefore increasing the earnings for the common stockholders.

Investments for "Growth"
Common Stock

Stock represents ownership in a company. There are two primary classes of stock: common and preferred.

Common stockholders participate in the earnings of the corporation through dividends declared by the board of directors and any capital gains made from the increase in the market value of the firm's stock. Dividends may be paid in cash, stock, or property. Common stockholders have the right to vote on company matters, which includes electing the management of the company.

Stock may be classified as blue chip, penny, income, growth, defensive, and cyclical. Blue chip stocks are large, established companies that have a longer record of profitable growth, dividend pay-out, and quality management. It includes names such as *Coca-Cola, GM, IBM*, and *McDonald's*. These stocks attract conservative investors because of their low volatility and steady dividends. The drawback is that they provide relatively little capital appreciation. Blue chip stocks are included in the Dow Jones Industrial Average, which is an index, compromised of 30 companies that are all major players in their respective industries. The DJIA accounts for about 1/5 of the total market value of all United States stocks. Penny stocks are low priced, speculative stocks that have a high degree of risk. They are normally small/new companies with a short and/or erratic history. Penny stocks usually sell for less than $5 per share.

Income stocks are focused on paying higher-than-average dividends. These primarily include utility and telephone companies. These are for investors who want a steady income stream. Growth stocks very seldom pay any dividends, since their goal is capital appreciation. The most growth potential is in the small and mid-sized companies.

Defensive stocks are those whose price stays stable when the market declines and are not adversely affected by cyclical fluctuations. In fact, these industries do quite well during a recession or a bear market. These are stocks issued by utility companies, food companies, tobacco, and alcohol companies. Cyclical stocks are just the opposite. They move up and down in sync with the business cycle. Some examples include the housing industry, automotive and industrial equipment companies. Investors who enjoy buying and selling as the market fluctuates tend to like these types of stocks. Conversely, long term investors prefer to avoid cyclical stocks because of their volatility.

Equities may be divided into small-cap, mid-cap, or large-cap based on their size (market capitalization). Small-caps are companies that have 1 billion or less in capitalization. Due to market growth, there's a sub-category called micro-cap for those companies with 400 million or less in capitalization. Mid-caps range from 2 - 4 billion in capitalization and large-cap start at 5 billion.

Mutual Funds

A mutual fund is a special kind of investment company called an "open-end" investment company. It is a company that makes investments on behalf of individuals and institutions which share common financial goals. The idea behind the mutual fund is simple. People pool their money in an effort to increase their buying power. Each fund manager will direct the placement of assets according to the stated investment objectives. This creates a portfolio of securities. An investor converts his dollars into shares of the portfolio. Each share represents ownership in all the securities and holdings of the fund. Each investor shares proportionately in both the gains and losses that the fund experiences. The specific type of securities purchased will be determined by the fund's investment manager. All pertinent information about a fund may be found in its prospectus.

A mutual fund is "open-ended" which allows investors to purchase or sell an unlimited amount of shares on any business day. A mutual fund is not a "stock" or "bond" per se, but it is a systematic method of investing and accumulating shares of a professionally managed diversified portfolio of securities.

Advantages of Mutual Funds

- Diversification. Each mutual fund holds a number of securities, sometimes hundreds. A level of diversification that few investors could achieve on their own. Spreading assets among many securities, reduces the risk of loss;
- Professional Management. Professional managers have access to extensive research, market information, skilled traders, and up to the minute in-depth data on market trends. They exhibit day to day "hands-on" management in an attempt to meet the fund's objectives in accordance with guidelines set forth in the prospectus. Few individual investors have the time and expertise to screen and evaluate the thousands of securities available daily in the financial markets;
- Marketability. Mutual fund shares may be bought or sold at any time. A fund is required to redeem shares of its portfolio each business day for the NAV (net asset value). Shares fluctuate in value in response to the general interest rate movement;
- Affordability. Most mutual funds have low investment minimums, which make them accessible to nearly everyone. For the first time, people who have a small amount of money to invest can gain access to the same portfolios as the wealthy;
- Flexibility. Mutual fund companies generally do not offer only one fund, but a variety of funds through its "family" of funds. Each of the professionally managed portfolios has different investment goals. This enables the investor to switch portfolios (normally without a charge) if there is a change in investment objectives;
- Easy Record Keeping. Funds provide quarterly statements, which make performance easy to monitor, and simplifies

paperwork during tax season. The important items to retain are all confirmations of purchases and redemptions, year-end account statements, and any 1099-Div or 1099-B forms;

- <u>Convenience</u>. Mutual funds may be purchased over the phone or by mail. Money may easily be transferred from one portfolio to another as needed. Contributions may be systematically deducted from a checking account and liquidations may be deposited into a checking or savings account. Any dividends or interest may be reinvested at no charge or paid to the investor either monthly or quarterly. Some funds offer check writing privileges;

- <u>Dollar cost averaging.</u> By systematically investing regularly, either directly via bank draft or by mail, the investor can automatically utilize and take advantage of the benefits of dollar cost averaging.

Disadvantages of Mutual Funds

- <u>No Guarantees.</u> Even though mutual funds may be purchased at a bank, or other financial institution, they are not guaranteed or insured by the bank, FDIC (Federal Deposit Insurance Corporation), or any other government agency. Fund shares are interest sensitive, therefore at liquidation, the investor may receive more or less than the original amount invested; and

- <u>Diversification Penalty.</u> While diversification may help eliminate the risk of a catastrophic loss associated with investing in an individual security, it also precludes the potential for a big gain that is only possible from owning an individual stock, which has the potential to experience a dramatic increase in value.

Categories of Mutual Funds In A Typical Family of Funds Include:

Aggressive Growth Funds
Small Cap Funds
Balanced Funds

Corporate Bond Funds
Global Funds
International Funds
Index Funds
Mid-Cap Funds
Government Funds
Growth Funds
Growth & Income Funds
High Yield Funds

Municipal Bond Funds
Money Market Funds
Utility Funds
Gold Funds
Natural Resource Funds
Foreign Stock Funds

Investments for "Special Situations"

Gold and Precious Metals

The value of gold and other precious metals is based on the fact that the supply is limited and the demand is constant. Historically, gold has been a solid value and a trusted medium of exchange. Purchasing gold and other precious metals is a way to diversify your investment portfolio. When traditional investments are doing poorly, gold, which often moves in the opposite direction, can help to stabilize your portfolio's value. Gold is primarily viewed as a hedge against inflation. The purchasing power of gold has remained fairly stable even in countries where paper money has become worthless and inflation has been out of control. Generally speaking, it is certainly within the parameters of prudent financial planning to have up to 10% of your assets invested in gold and/or precious metals.

Gold can also play an important role in retirement planning. The American Eagle gold coins are now eligible for inclusion in IRAs and other retirement programs.

Here are some of the most common ways to invest in gold:

- <u>Gold Certificates.</u> These represent ownership of gold bullion held for convenience and safety by a financial institution. There is a fee for both storage and insurance;
- <u>Gold Stock.</u> Stocks in individual gold mining companies which are traded on one or more stock exchanges. These can be volatile;
- <u>Gold Futures and Options.</u> Future contracts traded on one of the future exchanges, hedged with options;
- <u>Gold Mutual Fund.</u> Professionally managed diversified portfolio of gold stocks. Probably the safest method of investing in gold;
- <u>Gold Bullion.</u> The purchase of actual gold bars up to 400 ounces;
- <u>Gold Coins.</u> The most popular are the one ounce coins such as the American Eagle, Canadian Maple Leaf, and the South African Krugerrand. These are easy to buy and store;
- <u>Gold Jewelry.</u> This represents the largest consumption of gold each year;
- <u>Numismatic Gold Coins.</u> Normally valued by the amount of gold included in the coin.

If you are considering investing in gold, be sure to compare prices using leading coin publications, seek advice from local reputable dealers, and beware of telemarketing schemes. Take possession of your purchases and store them in a secure location.

Collectables

This includes investing in such items as art, antiques, coins, and stamps. Investing in collectables is typically an outgrowth of a personal interest or hobby. Normally, an investor should be very cautious about investing in any kind of collectable unless one has a specialized knowledge in that area. This is one of the riskiest forms of investing with uncertain returns and questionable liquidity. Most of the "yield" on collectables includes the personal enjoyment of ownership.

Commodities

Investing in commodities is essentially investment in raw materials. The market for commodity contracts is divided into four segments: grains and oilseeds; livestock and meat; food and fiber; and metals and petroleum. Being highly specialized, commodities are traded on their own exclusive exchanges. Investing in commodity futures, which promise to pay a given amount at some future date in the hope that the price at that particular time will be higher than you agreed, is even more specialized. Trading commodities requires a great amount of time and attention on the part of the investor. It is very intense and a fast paced environment. This type of investment is usually inappropriate for the unsophisticated investor, unless purchased through a mutual fund.

Oil and Gas Programs

There are three types of oil and gas programs: exploratory, developmental, and income. Exploratory or wildcatting is looking for undiscovered oil and gas reserves. There is potential for great reward, but this is also very risky. In the developmental program, drilling is done near existing fields to discover new reserves. It is a little less risky, however, few wells are actually produced. The income program has the lowest risk and provides immediate income to the investor from existing oil wells.

Diversification

One of the methods used to maintain the purchasing power of your money is diversification. This simply means to spread your money out and utilize different types of investment vehicles. It's the same concept expressed in the old adage, "Don't put all your eggs in one basket"!

There are three basic types of diversification. Diversification of an individual investment, diversification within each major investment category, and diversification among the major investment categories. Here's an example of each.

- *Diversification of **an individual** investment* (for a corporate bond) would be to: purchase shares of a corporate bond mutual fund; or purchase several different individual corporate bonds.
- *Diversification **within** a major investment category* (using the income category) would be to: purchase shares of corporate bond mutual fund, government securities mutual fund, and a Ginnie Mae mortgage mutual fund; or purchase an individual corporate bond, and individual government bond, and an individual Ginnie Mae mortgage.
- *Diversification **among** the major investment categories* is commonly known as asset allocation. This topic will be discussed in the next chapter.

The purpose of diversification is to maximize your return and reduce your overall risk exposure. Be careful not to *over diversify* to the point of ineffectiveness.

Portfolio Diversification

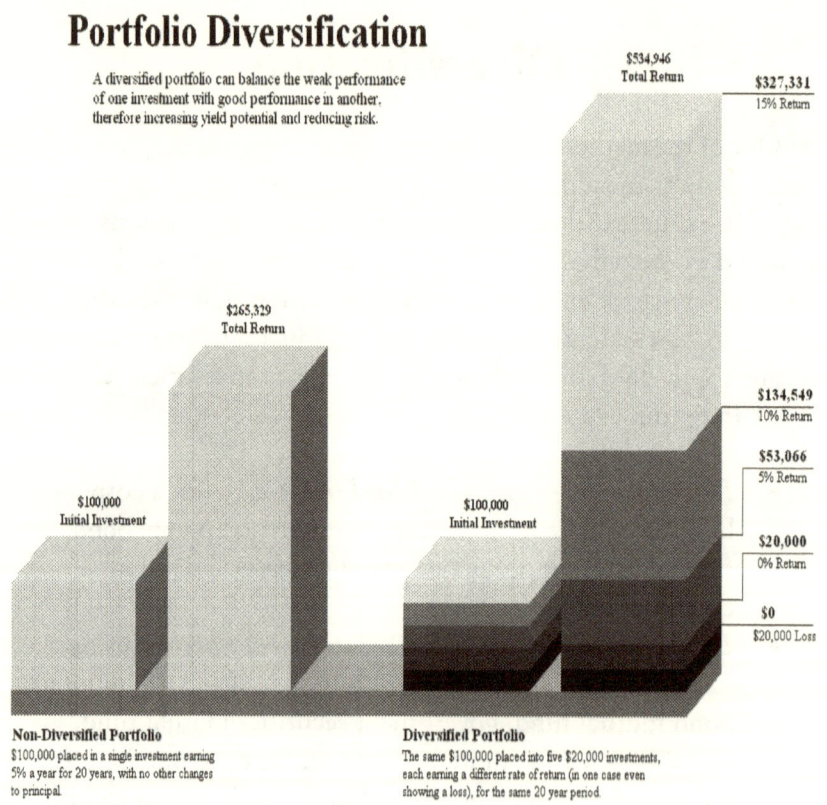

A diversified portfolio can balance the weak performance of one investment with good performance in another, therefore increasing yield potential and reducing risk.

$534,946
Total Return

$327,331
15% Return

$265,329
Total Return

$134,549
10% Return

$53,066
5% Return

$100,000
Initial Investment

$100,000
Initial Investment

$20,000
0% Return

$0
$20,000 Loss

Non-Diversified Portfolio
$100,000 placed in a single investment earning 5% a year for 20 years, with no other changes to principal.

Diversified Portfolio
The same $100,000 placed into five $20,000 investments, each earning a different rate of return (in one case even showing a loss), for the same 20 year period.

Total return for a particular period is the ending redeemable value of the initial investment at the end of the period shown, assuming annual reinvestment of all income. The returns shown are hypothetical and do not represent the returns of any particular investment or investments. Actual returns on any particular investment will depend on the particular market factors and risks applicable to that investment.

Asset Allocation

Asset allocation is a special type of diversification. This strategy involves diversifying your money among the three major investment categories.

Factors such as your investment objectives, age, tolerance for risk, and time parameters should be considered in determining the percentage of assets allocated to each investment category to make sure that it is appropriate for your situation.

Over time, asset allocation can have a profound effect on the performance of your investment portfolio. This sophisticated form of diversification can help to maximize your returns while managing your exposure to risk. One study found that asset allocation can account for over 90% of a portfolio's performance. While market timing, which is buying and selling an investment at the most favorable time, and the selection of specific securities account for less than 10% of a portfolios overall return. Institutional investors have been successfully using asset allocation for years.

The purpose of asset allocation is to help protect your money against "market risk" by positioning your investments in such a way that regardless of how the market moves, some portion, of your investments is making money! One of the critical aspects of asset allocation is portfolio rebalancing. This is the periodic (usually quarterly or semi-annually) re-allocation of the portfolio's assets back to the original asset mix. Money is taken from the better performing investments and put into the relative under performing investments. There are several advantages to this strategy:

- Easy to implement;
- Helps maintain a constant risk level;
- Allows balanced diversification to be maintained;
- Precludes the portfolio from becoming over- weighted in equities at market highs and under- weighted at market lows.

Annual evaluations are necessary to ensure that the investor's established risk tolerance level and expectations have not changed.

The amount of money that you place into each category will vary depending on your tolerance for market risk. Your tolerance for market risk is measured by your risk profile.

Risk Profile Questionnaire

You can get a general idea of your risk profile by answering the following questions.

1. Which strategy would you select if you were purchasing a house?
   a) Get a monthly payment which easily fits within your budget;
   b) Fit the payment into your budget, but make the smallest down payment, using the extra funds for investing;
   c) Go for the biggest mortgage you can afford.

2. How many years before you expect to retire?
   a) Less than 5 years;
   b) 5 to 10 years;
   c) 11 to 20 years +.

3. Recognizing that by taking additional risk you have the potential for increasing investment results you would:
   a) Be unlikely to take any more risk;
   b) Be willing to take a little more risk with some of your money;
   c) Be willing to accept more risk with all of your money.

4. Some of your savings is in a mutual fund which has climbed steadily for 8 months, then drops 25% in one month, would you:
   a) Sell ASAP;
   b) Sell half-keep the rest;
   c) Stay put and consider buying more shares.

5. You've saved $8,000 to buy your newborn son a car when he reaches 18. Realizing that a new car will probably cost three times more by then, you:
   a) Decide to forget it;
   b) Set aside another $8,000;
   c) Invest in a growth mutual fund.

Determine your score- A=1; B=2; C=3

    5-8   =   Conservative
    9-12 =   Moderate
    13-15 =   Aggressive

Which type of investor are you?

Here are the recommended asset percentages for each of the major investment categories, as profiled for the "conservative," "moderate," and "aggressive" investor. Use these models as a guide for allocating your money. There are numerous variations possible.

A conservative investor seeks to avoid market risk and is primarily interested in income and capital preservation. The usual age range is 65 and older. Please note that even the most conservative investor has at least 10% of his assets in the growth category.

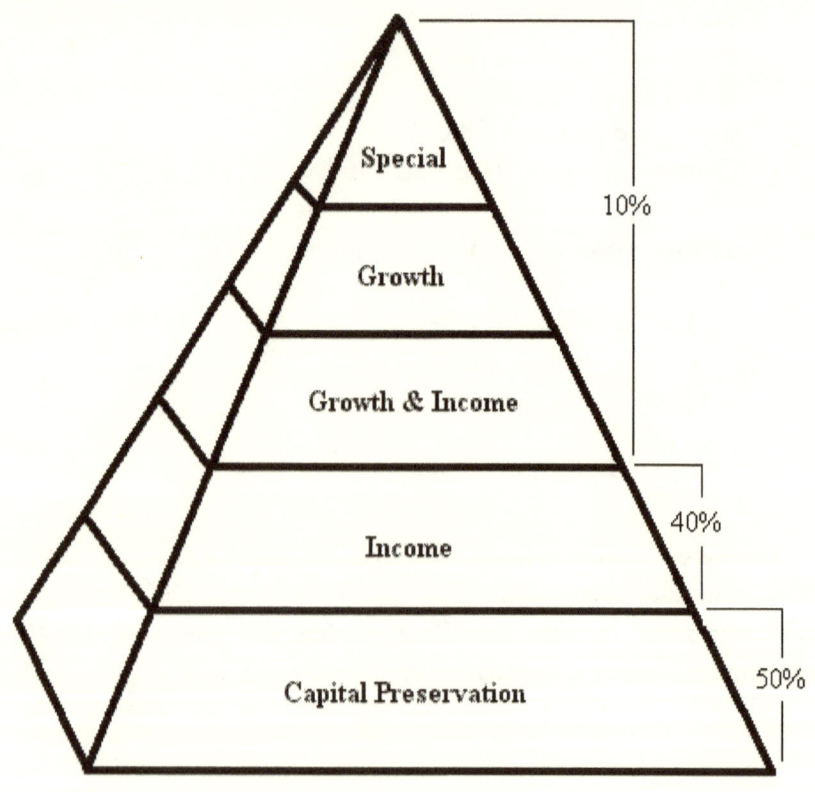

"Conservative" Approach

10% Growth
40% Income
50% Cash

The moderate investor (age 45-60) generally seeks returns that will out pace inflation and can accept some year-to-year fluctuation in pursuit of long-term objectives. The moderate investor wants "controlled" risk.

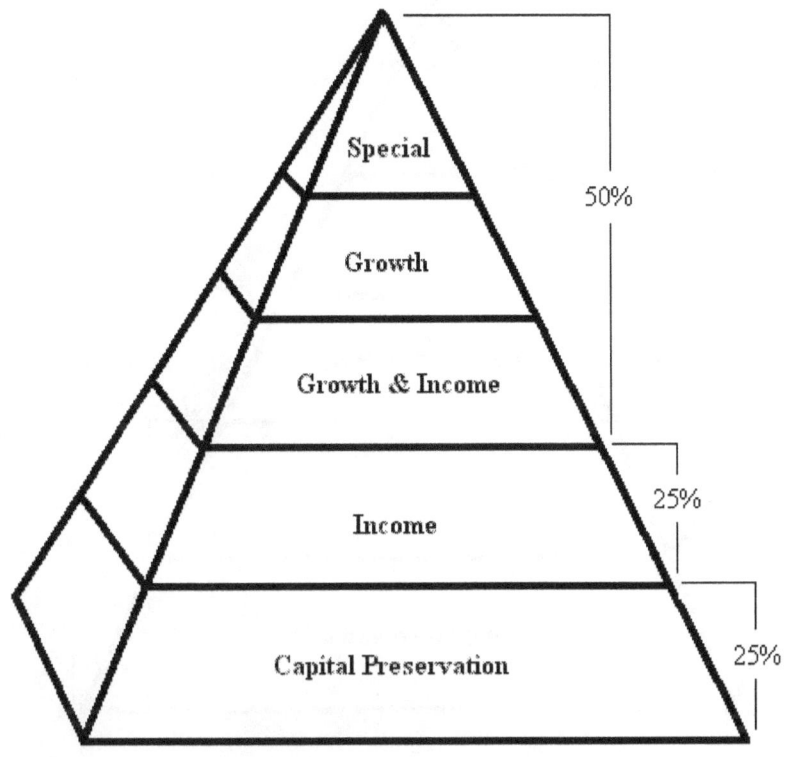

"Moderate" Approach

50% Growth
25% Income
25% Cash

The aggressive investor is willing to accept significant market risk in order to gain maximum investment growth. The usual age range for this group is 20's to 40's.

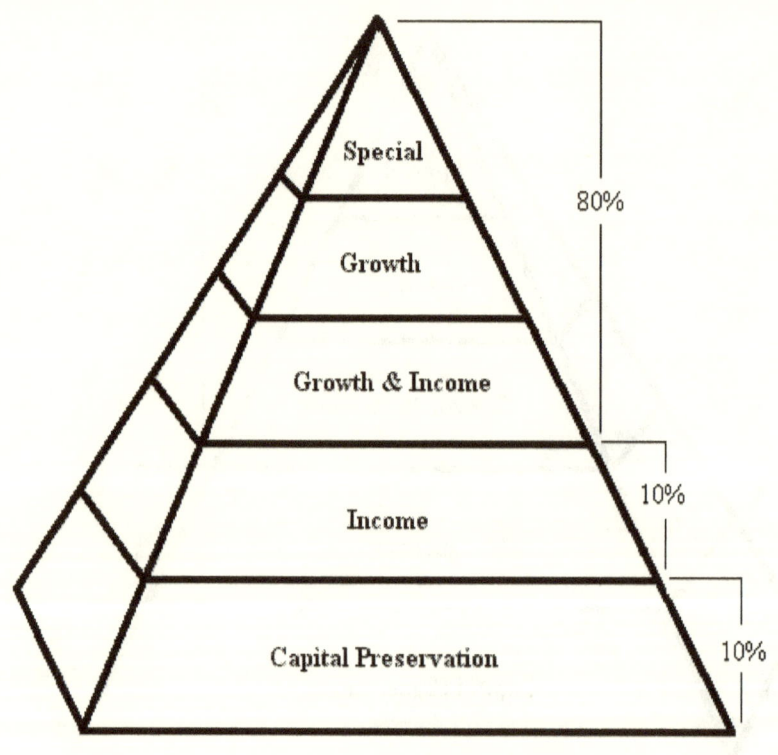

"Aggressive" Approach

80% Growth
10% Income
10% Cash

A common concern of many investors is how to determine the appropriate amount of money that they should put into the "growth" category. The answer depends upon your age.

The "Rule of Thumb" is to subtract your current age from 100 and this will equal the acceptable and prudent percent of your money suitable for the growth category. For example, if you are age 60, and 40% of your assets were in "growth" investments, then you would be within the parameters of prudent financial planning. This is only a guideline. The most important aspect of investing is that you must be comfortable with the investments you select. The actual amount put into the growth category will vary depending upon the investor's unique circumstances.

Remember, no one can completely eliminate all investment risk! There is no risk-free investment. There is no "perfect" or "best" investment. All investment decisions are a compromise. Nothing remains constant, which is why investments need to be monitored and revised from time to time.

The Rule of 72

You've probably heard of the Rule of 72. This is a method for estimating how long it will take for an investment to double in value. Simply divide 72 by the interest rate or rate of return. The result is the approximate number of years that it will take for your money to double in value.

For example, if you invest $10,000 at 10% interest, it should double to $20,000 in about 7.2 years.

$$(72 \div 10 = 7.2)$$

You can also determine the rate of return for an investment if you divide 72 by the number of years it took for your money to double in value. If it took 12 years for your money to double then you were earning about 6%.

$$(72 \div 12 = 6)$$

The Rule of 108

What most people don't realize is that the Rule of 72 hypothetical was designed for tax-deferred or tax-exempt investments such as annuities or municipal bonds.

The calculation for taxable investments is different. To figure approximately how long it would take to double your money in a taxable investment, you use the Rule of 108. Simply divide 108 by the interest rate/rate of return and it will give you the approximate number of years that it will take for you to double the value of your money.

A taxable investment earning 6% would double in value in about 18 years.

$$(108 \div 6 = 18)$$

Likewise, if it took 12 years to double the value of your money, you could surmise that you were earning about 9%.

$$(108 \div 12 = 9)$$

You can also use the Rule of 108 to illustrate the effects of inflation by calculating the time period in which the price of goods and services will double. Divide 108 by the annual inflation rate based on the CPI (Consumer Price Index). This will give you the number of years that it will take for prices to double. For example, if the annual inflation rate is 6%, then a loaf of bread, which now costs $1.50, should cost $3.00 in about 18 years (108 $\div$ 6 = 18). Remember, this is only an estimate.

Please keep in mind that the Rule of 72 and the Rule of 108 assume that the investor is in the 33% tax bracket.

Dollar Cost Averaging

There has been a lot of talk about dollar cost averaging. There seems to be some misconceptions about this strategy. Dollar cost averaging is systematically investing a fixed dollar amount at regular intervals----weekly, monthly, or quarterly, over a given period of time without regard to share price. When prices are low, more shares are acquired for the same number of dollars than when prices are high. Your average cost per share should always be lower than the simple average of the share prices during the period in which the purchases were made. (See chart below)

This technique will not protect you against possible losses if the market makes a sudden severe correction. You must be disciplined enough to keep investing during temporary corrections in order for the law of averages to work effectively. Fluctuations in the market are a part of the dollar cost averaging methodology.

For those who have a lump sum to invest, the decision has to be made whether to invest all the money into the market at one time or to invest using dollar cost averaging. The answer really depends upon how the market is moving. If the market is in a gradual declining trend or is fairly volatile (going up for a few days and then swinging downward for a few days) dollar cost averaging would be effective. However, if the market is in a gradual rising trend, then it could actually work against you. In this case, it might be better to invest in the market all at one time.

Before you use dollar cost averaging or any other investment strategy, I encourage you to consult your investment advisor.

Fluctuating Market

The hypothetical illustration below assumes you have made regular investments of $100 per quarter.

Quarter	Regular Investment	Price Per Share	Shares Purchased
1	$100	$10	10
2	$100	$5	20
3	$100	$10	10
4	$100	$5	20
Total	$400		60

Average cost per share: $6.67 ($400 ÷ 60 shares)
Average price per share: $7.50
                    ($10 + $5 + $10 + $5 = $30 ÷ 4 purchases)
The offering prices paid each quarter (shown above) equaled the average share price for that quarter. The prices shown are hypothetical and do not reflect the performance of any particular investment. Steady investing does not assure a profit or protect against loss in declining markets. You should consider your financial ability to continue purchases through periods of low price levels.

Types of Investment Risk

Risk is a natural and central element of investing. Since risk can not be eliminated, investors need to learn how to manage it. By diversifying investments, appropriately allocating assets, as well as establishing a prudent financial plan, an investor will be able to develop risk -control strategies that will enable him to achieve his objectives. There is a misperception among investors that risk is bad. In reality, the greatest risk for investors is taking no risk at all! One of the biggest challenges for investors will always be the ability to manage risk effectively.

Effective risk management begins with a thorough understanding of its various forms and the potential impact that it can have on a portfolio. Investment risk may be broadly defined as the probability that the _actual_ return from an investment will differ from its _expected_ return. The _total_ risk of an investment may be divided into two categories: non-diversifiable risk and diversifiable risk. Non-diversifiable risk (sometimes called _systematic_ risk) refers to that portion of total variability in return caused by factors affecting the prices of _all_ comparable investments. Diversifiable risk is the portion of the risk that is unique to a firm, industry, or property. It represents the segment of investment risk that may be reduced through diversification.

The following chart classifies the major types of investment risk by category, defines each risk, and shows which kinds of investments are affected by that risk.

Non-Diversifiable

Risk type	Definition	Investment Affected
1. Market Risk	Risk that the investment value will rise or fall with general market movements	Stocks, Bonds
2. Interest Rate Risk	Risk that the value of an investment will fluctuate in response to changes in general level of interest rates	Preferred Stock, Mortgage-Back Securities, Fixed Annuities, Bonds
3. Purchasing Power Risk (Inflation Risk)	Risk that money will lose its purchasing power overtime as costs of goods and services rise	Preferred Stock, Mortgage-Back Securities, Fixed Annuities, Bonds, CDs, MMA

Diversifiable

Risk type	Definition	Investment Affected
1. Credit Risk	The risk that the issuing company may not be able to meet it's financial obligations	Fixed Annuity, Corporate and Municipal Bonds
2. Reinvestment Risk	The risk that the cash distributions from an investment can't be reinvested at the same rate of return as the original investment	Bonds, Mortgages, Limited Partnerships
3. Business Risk	The risk that a particular company will fail (due to poor management, inadequate product demand, etc.)	Stocks, Municipal and Corporate Bonds, REIT, Annuity
4. Industry Risk	The risk that a particular industry will be adversely affected despite a strong general economy	Stocks and Bonds

5. Economic Risk	The risk that the economy will slow down or enter a recession, depressing corporate earnings	Stocks, Bonds, and Real Estate
6. Liquidity Risk	The risk that an investment can't be turned quickly into cash	Real Estate Limited Partnerships, Annuities
7. Currency Risk	The risk that an investment could be adversely affected by the exchange rate between the U.S. and foreign currency	International Securities, U.S. companies doing business overseas
8. Political Risk	The risk that a government could nationalize private industry or be overthrown	International Securities, U.S. companies doing business in foreign countries

There are three additional types of risk not listed on the chart. They are market-timing risk, shortfall risk, and emotional risk. Let's briefly discuss each one.

Market-timing risk is the risk associated with trying to time the market for buying and selling securities. Jumping in and out of the market in an attempt to anticipate ups and downs is risky business. The solution to this type of risk is very simple. Just invest for the long term and don't be influenced by daily market hype. Making changes in your portfolio based on what you think the market will do next can cause severe losses. In addition, you could be out of the market on its best performing days. Assume an individual invested $10,000 in U.S. stocks (represented by the S&P 500) for 10 years ending June 30, 2002.

Look at the results: (Returns include reinvested dividends.)

- Stayed invested entire period $29,509
- Missed 5 best days...$23,266
- Missed 10 best days...$19,175
- Missed 20 best days...$13,784
  Source: *Standard & Poor's*

Shortfall risk is the risk that an investment portfolio does not meet an investor's financial needs. Several things can cause this to happen, such as a sudden need for cash, or perhaps living longer than anticipated. Without proper planning these issues could causes problems. One of the best ways to avoid shortfall risk is to keep an emergency fund equal to at least six months living expenses for unplanned events and urgent cash demands. Also, another way to avoid shortfall risk is to anticipate future cash needs such as a child's college education expenses and invest some of your money conservatively for the short term, so that it will be easily accessible.

Emotional risk is the risk that an investment decision will be influenced by emotional factors. Greed and fear are the two most prevalent, followed closely by pride and regret. These emotions can lead to poor decisions and consequently portfolio losses. It's important to understand your investments, but it's equally important to understand yourself and especially your tolerance for risk. As an investor, you must be comfortable with your decisions and have a <u>logical</u> decision making process.

It should be obvious at this point that <u>all</u> investments have some type of risk. Since risk <u>cannot</u> be avoided, it must be ***managed***.

Personal Investment Plan

Based on your investment objective, create your own personal investment plan. (You might want to review pages 4-9 before you begin.) Decide how you want to invest your money using the worksheets and the investment pyramid strategy. Simply follow these 5 steps:

Step 1   **Developing an Investment Plan**

- Complete Worksheet I

Step 2   **Calculating Your Net Worth**

- Complete Worksheet II

Step 3   **Determining Monthly Surplus**

- Complete Worksheet III

- Find Money for Investing
  (already saved, sell an asset, systematically accumulate)

Step 4   **Completing the Investment Pyramid**
(Worksheet IV)

- State and write-in your investment objective
(capital preservation/income/growth&income/
growth/speculation)

- Select suitable investments after determining
risk tolerance level and considering investment
parameters

- Write-in investments within appropriate categories
of the investment pyramid using the conservative,
moderate, or aggressive approach allocations as a
guide

Step 5   **Purchasing Investments!**

- Use discount or full service brokerage

- Purchase through your investment advisor

Worksheet I

Developing an Investment Plan

What are your investment goals? (Be specific)

	Target Date	Estimated Cost	Amount Needed to Save Monthly
*Short Term Goals: (1 Year)			
1.)			
2.)			
3.)			
4.)			
5.)			
*Intermediate Goals: (2-4 Years)			
1.)			
2.)			
3.)			
4.)			
5.)			
*Long Term Goals: (5+ Years)			
1.)			
2.)			
3.)			
4.)			
5.)			

*list in order of importance

Worksheet II

Net Worth Calculation

Assets		Liabilities	
Personal Bank Accounts	_____	Mortgage Balance	_____
Certificates of Deposit	_____	Other Real Estate Loans	_____
Investments:		Car Loan Balance	_____
Stock	_____	Credit Card Balance	_____
Bonds	_____	Student Loan(s) Balance	_____
Preferred Stock	_____	Other Loans	_____
Real Estate			
(Market Value)	_____	Taxes (annual)	_____
Business Interest	_____	Outstanding Debt	_____
Other	_____	Other Bills/Obligations	_____
Home		Other	_____
(Market Value)	_____		
Retirement Plans:			
IRA	_____		
401k/403b	_____		
Keogh/SEP	_____		
Profit Sharing	_____		
Pension	_____		
Life Insurance			
(Cash Value)	_____		
Annuities	_____		
Personal Property			
(Jewelry/paintings/etc.)	_____		
Inheritance	_____		
Trust	_____		
Other	_____		

Total Assets: _____   Total Liabilities: _____

Total Assets   _____

— (Subtract)

Total Liabilities   _____

NET WORTH   _____

Worksheet III

Monthly Surplus Calculation

Gross Monthly Income   Monthly Expenses

Gross Monthly Income				Monthly Expenses	
Salary	_____	Income Taxes	_____	Credit Cards	_____
Commissions	_____	Housing:		Meals out	_____
Bonuses	_____	Mort/Rent	_____	Entertainment	_____
Tips	_____	Insurance	_____	Baby Sitter	_____
Interest	_____	Taxes	_____	Trips	_____
Dividends	_____	Elect/Gas	_____	Vacations	_____
Rental Property	_____	Water	_____	Clubs	_____
Social Security	_____	Sewer	_____	Clothing	_____
Annuities	_____	Telephone	_____	Doctor	_____
Retirement Plan	_____	Maintenance	_____	Dentist	_____
Alimony	_____	Other	_____	Drugs	_____
Child Support	_____	Food	_____	Medical	_____
Trust	_____	Auto:		Misc.	_____
Other	_____	Insurance	_____	Personal Items	_____
		Loan Pmt	_____	Tuition	_____
		Tag	_____	Allowance	_____
		Gas	_____	Laundry	_____
		Maintenance	_____	Lunches	_____
		Insurance:		Gifts	_____
		Life	_____	Other	_____
		Health	_____	Child Care	_____
		Disability	_____	Education	_____
		Other Ins.	_____	Savings	_____
		Investment	_____		
		Retirement:			
		401k/403b	_____		
		IRA	_____		

Total Monthly Income _____ **Total Monthly Expenses** _____

> **Total Monthly Income**   _____
>   **— (Subtract)**
> **Total Monthly Expenses**   _____
> **Monthly Surplus***   _____

*The entire monthly surplus should be used for investing only after establishing an emergency fund equal to six months living expenses, and having purchased adequate life, health, disability, and property insurance to protect your family against financial loss. Your goal should be to save at <u>least</u> 10% of your take-home pay each month.

The Investment Pyramid

Investment Objective:

_____

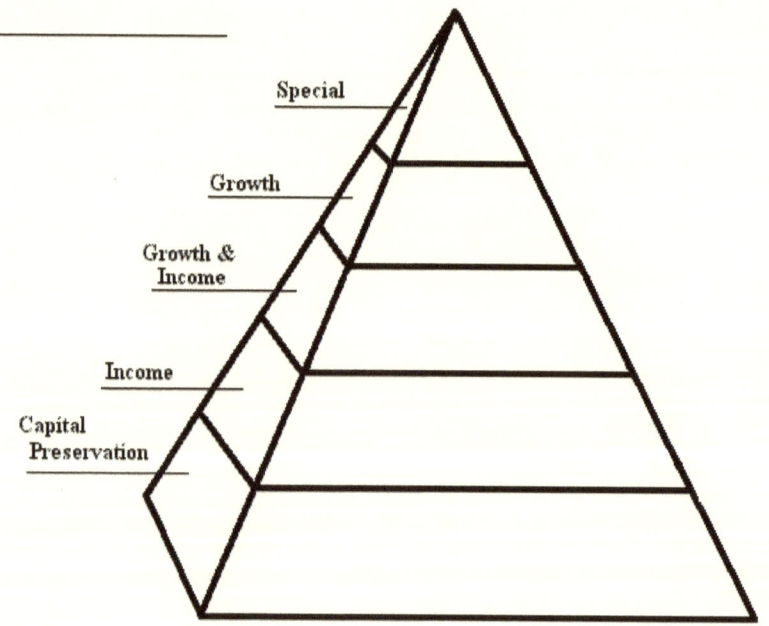

Special

Growth

Growth &
Income

Income

Capital
Preservation

Personal Investment Plan

Key Points to Remember

1. Choose investments congruent with your financial objectives, risk tolerance level, and time parameters.
2. Diversify. Use asset allocation and portfolio rebalancing.
3. Remember equities need an 8-10 year time period for best results. It's crucial to stay invested. Time *in the market* is what is important.
4. Don't panic or get upset over daily market hype. Stay focused on your goals.
5. Short-term the market goes up and down, but the long-term trend has been upward. Think long-term.
6. You must be able to tolerate market volatility if you want higher returns. The market rewards patience and punishes impatience.
7. A portfolio matched to your goals in life is an *investment*. A portfolio driven by market outlook is *speculation*.
8. If you do not understand an investment then it's risky!
9. Review your program at least annually. Make any necessary changes.
10. Consider consulting a professional financial advisor when needed.

Don't Procrastinate!

The most important factor is to get started immediately. Do not put it off! Look at ***The Price of Procrastination*** graph on the following page to see the consequences of waiting. You must be accountable for your actions and take control of your financial situation. The biggest obstacle to an effective investment program is procrastination. Do not try to "time the market"…you can't!

The very best time to invest is always right now. It's up to you to make it happen.

Just do it!

The Price of Procrastination

This graph shows how much would have to be invested each month to accumulate $250,000 assuming that twelve equal payments are made in a savings program per year, earning 8% per annum compounded monthly over the periods 5, 10, 20, and 30 years respectively.

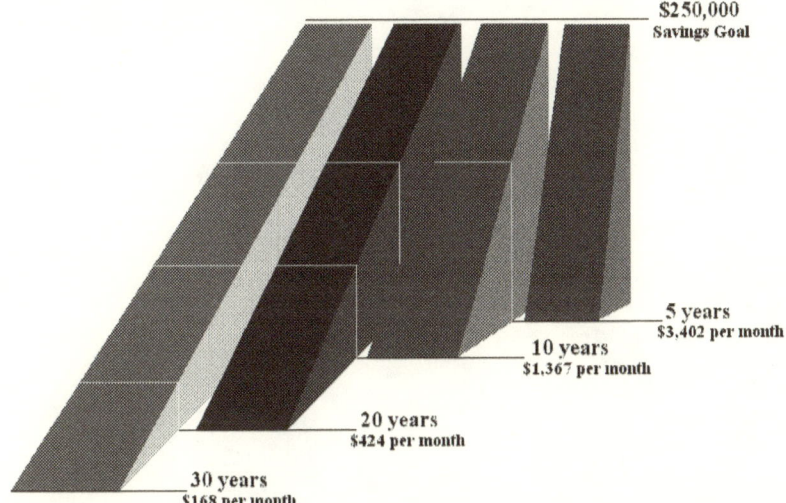

$250,000
Savings Goal

5 years
$3,402 per month

10 years
$1,367 per month

20 years
$424 per month

30 years
$168 per month

Periodic investing in investments subject to market value fluctuations does not assure a profit nor protect against loss in declining markets. These examples assume that there is no fluctuation in principal value, and do not take into account any tax obligations as to income or earnings. These examples are hypothetical and do not depict or predict investment returns of any particular investment.

Glossary

Bear Market   a severe decline in the market of 20% or more; usually associated with falling prices, investor pessimism, economic slow down, and government restraint

Capital Preservation protection against negative developments while taking advantage of positive developments; used when referring to guaranteed investments

Coupon   defines the amount of annual interest income paid by a bond

Dividend   periodic payment made by a corporation to its shareholders from past or current earnings

Equity   represents ownership in a specific business or property; used to refer to common stock

Index   numbers used to measure the general price behavior of a representative group of stocks in relation to a base value set at an earlier point in time

Liquidity   feature of an investment to be readily convertible into cash

Marginal Tax Rate   the tax rate on additional income

Maturity Date   the date on which a security matures and the principal is repaid

Par   face amount of a security

Pass-through   type of mortgage-backed security where the income is paid to the investor until mortgage is paid off

Principal	amount of capital that must be paid at maturity; Original amount invested
Pro Rata	proportionate allocation
Rider	an addition to a document (policy), such as an annuity; it may be used to increase a basic benefit or delete a benefit
Unit	basic quantity of purchase for a unit investment trust or an annuity
Yield	the percentage return from an investment

NOTES

NOTES

NOTES